Autism and Me

Sibling Stories

Ouisie Shapiro   Photographs by Steven Vote

Albert Whitman & Company, Morton Grove, Illinois

Dear Reader,

This book is filled with stories of kids I have interviewed. They want you to meet their brothers and sisters, who have a condition called autism. This means that their brains work in a different way from other people's brains.

There are many ideas about what causes autism, but no one knows for sure. Some scientists think that some kids might have autism because it runs in their families. But knowing the exact cause of autism is hard because the human brain is very complicated.

If you have a sister or brother with autism, you know that their behaviors are different from those of other kids. They don't always like to be around other people—even people in their own families. Some people with autism like to do the same thing over and over. They may make noises that sound strange to other people, or flap their arms in a funny way. Many of them

are unable to talk, so they can't say what they want or how they feel.

Just because kids have autism doesn't mean they don't have fun. The brothers and sisters in this book do lots of things together. They play in the snow, blow bubbles, and read stories. My niece Arie has autism. She and her brother Luke like to slide down the stairs together. But mostly, Arie likes to spend time alone, listening to her iPod or playing on the Barney web site.

Maybe you know kids at school or in your neighborhood who have autism. If you do, you may know that they have a hard time understanding what someone is saying. You can help kids with autism by not teasing them or letting other kids tease them. They deserve our respect.

I like reading to Ravi. We have fun!

Some people think kids like Ravi are stupid because they have trouble learning. That makes me mad. I'm proud of my brother.

He was two and a half when the doctors diagnosed him with autism. Ravi doesn't talk as well as other people. And he has odd behavior. Sometimes he just gets up and leaves the house. He used to freak out and throw things when we went to the mall. But now he's much better.

Ravi's in first grade. He goes to school, and he has an aide who stays with him all day. She sits

Amber & Ravi

next to him and helps him stay focused. And when Ravi doesn't understand what the classroom teacher is saying, the aide explains it to him. On Tuesdays, two teenagers from a group called Friendship Circle come to our house to spend time with Ravi. They help him learn how to play with other kids.

Ravi is always happy, and he's cool. He has an amazing memory. If he loses some-

thing, five weeks later he'll remember everything about it—what color it was, how big it was, what shape it was, and how it worked.

Ravi and I read together at bedtime. Sometimes I read from a book, and sometimes I make up a story and put him in it. If I make up a story about a boy who goes fishing, Ravi will help tell the story, too. He's smart and he tries hard, and he's come such a long way from where he was. He's my favorite person, and I wouldn't have him any other way.

Ron and I are like any other brother and sister. Sometimes we fight, but mostly we get along. Ron used to have behavior problems. He would bite me if he got frustrated. But he doesn't do that anymore. He doesn't get frustrated as much as he used to.

My mother calls him "the Mayor" because he talks to everybody. He walks up to people and says, "Hi, my name is Ron." He's really good with the kids on his basketball team. He encourages them when they get upset.

Ron is doing great in school. He has physical therapy for his fine motor skills. He's getting to where he can write words and we can read them. He knows his class

Pauline & Ron

schedule by heart. And he can tell you the school lunch menu for every day of the week! But if anything changes in his routine, he gets messed up. He was nine when we moved from our apartment to our house, and every day he said, "I want to go home. I want to sleep in my bed."

Transitions are the biggest problem for Ron. He'll be going to high school in the fall, and that will be scary. The building is so big, and it might be hard for him to cope with so many kids. I went to the same school, so I've been telling him what to expect. If I have to, I'll go to school with him until he feels comfortable. I don't want him to be afraid because of his autism.

My brother Ron likes it when I hug him.

Jack doesn't talk. It's hard to have autism.

My brother Jack has autism. Something is wrong with his brain, so he can't talk. Sometimes he says funny words that don't make sense. I talk for Jack. It's good to have him as a brother. I get to go on the Internet to find out about autism.

The money I made for selling Girl Scout cookies went to Autism Speaks. It's an organization that helps people with autism. I sold 300 boxes, the most of any other kid.

At school I wrote a story called "Jack and His Autism."

Amy & Jack

It's about how Jack makes funny signs with his fingers and people have no idea what it means.

When we go out to eat, Jack jumps up and down and makes lots of noises. It's okay with me. He's doing it because he has to.

My mom took us to a bookstore so I could get another Boxcar Children mystery. Jack held my mom's hand, and he didn't get lost or run out into the street. But when we went to a restaurant for lunch, he cried the whole time. Some people gave us mean dirty looks, and we had to go home. He has autism, what's the big deal?

Jack's in love with Helen. She goes to his school. At school Jack's learning potty training, and he's learning to use pictures so he can tell people what he wants.

It would be good if Jack could talk, but I really wish that he could run as fast as me and have good handwriting like me.

I'm like most kids, but my sister Arie is not.

It's hard to have a sister like Arie because sometimes in public she throws a tantrum and cries. So you have to be flexible when you go to the store or the playground. People with autism aren't typical, and they can't do stuff that typical kids can. I'm like most kids, but Arie's not. But kids with autism are not dumb or stupid, and you shouldn't treat them like they are.

I read a book for school about Helen Keller. She lived in a quiet world because

Luke & Arie

she couldn't hear or see or speak. Arie has all the senses that we have but she can't process what her senses tell her. She can say hi, but she can't have a conversation.

My mom thinks Arie only understands one word in a sentence. So if you say, "Arie, want to go to the bakery?" she only hears the word *bakery*. Sometimes Arie is smart. Like when my dad and I are getting ready to go outside to play catch, she sees me getting my baseball glove out of the closet, and she puts her shoes on.

During the week Arie lives at her school. It's called Evergreen. She goes there during the day and then stays at a house near the school. I think she would rather be at home. She can have more treats at home. She used to have a tantrum when she went back on Sunday, but now she leaves the house with a smile on her face.

When Arie gets older, I think she'll live in a home with other kids like her. I might take her out for Chinese food on Saturdays.

I can pick up Jeremy even though he's a strong little guy.

Autism makes my little brother Jeremy go nuts. He needs help with his behavior. He pushes people and punches them. And he likes to jump on top of me. I tell him not to, but he doesn't listen. He screams a lot. It's a disaster when other kids come to play with him!

Jeremy goes to a special school for kids with autism. He's the fastest runner in his class. And he's the smartest kid. He knows a lot of things. He's an expert at arts and crafts. He draws pictures of penguins and then cuts them out. He's very careful to cut along the edges. If I don't cut my picture exactly along the edge—and any white paper is showing—he gets upset and makes me start all over.

Anthony & Jeremy

I like sharing a room with Jeremy. He's good company. We sleep in bunk beds, and at night we get out of bed and sneak into the living room to get our toys. Sometimes Jeremy screams in the middle of the night, and my mom has to come in. But that's okay, I'm used to it.

Jeremy and I will be friends when we grow up. I think he'll be a firefighter 'cause he loves everything about them. He has little rubber ducks that are dressed like firefighters. When I grow up, I'm going to be a rock-'n'-roll singer. And I'll probably be a movie star, too.

I think Jeremy likes having a brother like me. He's happy to see me when I come home from school. He yells, "Anthony!" and he hugs and squeezes me to death!

Ford is happy now.
I hope he stays happy all his life.

I feel lucky to have a brother like Ford because I'm exposed to more things. One time we were at the beach, and we saw hermit crabs. Ford called them spiders, and I thought about how they *did* look like spiders. So he helps me see different points of view.

Ford doesn't understand about personal space. My best friend Emma came for a sleepover, and we were playing in my room. Ford came in without asking and was jumping on the bed with us. Then he took Emma's hand and said, "Go on computer, Emma." At first I didn't like that he came into my room. But in the end I told Emma that I was happy he did.

Callie & Ford

Ford's in a special needs class with six boys. The teachers are helping him have better behavior. He also has therapists who come to our house. They play with him and help him understand things better. I know learning takes time.

When he grows up, he's not going to have the kind of lifestyle that most adults have. My mom said I'm going to have to have a pullout couch or an extra bedroom so he can stay with me sometimes.

Every year for Ford's birthday we go on a trip. One year we went to Story Land in New Hampshire. Ford loved the roller coaster so much we went on it fifty-eight times in two and a half days!

Most people think autism is when you have no social skills. But Amaya is really social. She loves to sing and talk. She started talking when she was four, and she hasn't stopped since! My friends read books to her. And she loves to watch *Barney* and *Blues Clues*. Those shows have a lot of color and singing in them.

On holidays my mom and I go to California to visit my grandparents. I wish Amaya could go with us, but she doesn't like the airplane, so she stays home with my dad. She doesn't mind because she and my dad have fun together.

I think it would be really fun to be Amaya. She gets taken out all the time. After school different people come for home visits. They take Amaya to the mall, to the YMCA to swim, and to restaurants. And she doesn't have homework!

Deia & Amaya

Sometimes I get frustrated with Amaya. She likes to stick her hand in my face or pull my hair. If I tell her to stop, she won't. And when she doesn't want to do something, she flops on the floor and has a tantrum.

When Amaya gets aggressive she has to spend time in her room, because no one can be around her when she gets like that. I got my driver's license, so I'm

excited to spend time alone with her—without parents and teachers. I'm happy I can start doing more things for her. When she gets into an aggressive mood, going for an outing usually helps. She loves being in the car with me!

Amaya is sitting on my lap and talking, as usual.

My brother Sam has autism, but he's good at reading words.

Sam and I go to the same school. He's in third grade. He's two years older than me. Half the day he goes to a regular classroom, and the other half he goes to a classroom with other kids who have autism.

One day Sam gave the morning announcement to the whole school! He talks in a high voice, and people in my class were laughing at him. I was kind

Troy & Sam

of embarrassed. I told them to stop and the teacher did, too, but they didn't.

Sam bugs me a lot of the time. I don't allow him in my room. I have all my valuables in there. And he likes to rip things. I don't tell people about my brother. I only told my best friend, Ayaad, that Sam's different from us.

When Ayaad comes to my house, we don't usually play with Sam. Sam likes to play with his trucks. Ayaad and I do different stuff. Whenever Sam sees Ayaad, he says, "Ayaad, when's your birthday?" I say, "Stop it!" but he doesn't.

I wish Sam could talk more. If I ask him something, he doesn't answer. I think having autism is like being in a dark room and the light never turns on. I did that once. I turned out the light and pretended I couldn't turn it back on. It was really scary!

Jesse has autism, but he's much more social than I am!

My brother Jesse has autism, but I don't think to myself, Jesse has autism and he can't do things. I wouldn't want him to change. If he did change even one little thing, he wouldn't be Jesse anymore, and I would miss the old Jesse.

When we eat, Jesse has to have lemonade or he gets upset. So we can't eat Chinese food. One night we went to a restaurant. There was a long wait, and Jesse was screaming. We had to come home for forty-five minutes so he could relax, and then we drove back to the restaurant.

Jesse doesn't like to see me unhappy. If I'm crying, he brings me tissues and rubs my eyes and says, "Emma, are you sad?"

Emma & Jesse

Jesse is crazy about telephones. He has a box filled with old phones. He presses the buttons and pretends to talk. If he came to your house, he'd look all around for your phones, and he'd remember where they are and what color they are. If you changed any of your phones, he'd know right away. My doctor moved her fax machine from one room to another. Months later, when Jesse walked into the office, the first thing he said was, "Where's the fax machine?"

I told Jesse that in three years I'm going to go to college and after that I'll probably live in an apartment. He said, "When you have an apartment, will you have phones I can play with?"

My brother Justin has autism. His brain doesn't work like other people's brains. When I was little, my parents told me that Justin had trouble speaking and didn't listen a lot. Also, they said he doesn't understand what people are saying, and he can't follow directions.

Justin only likes certain foods, like Lorna Doones and peanut butter sandwiches and spaghetti. I wish he could say *spaghetti* better. He says "some-ghetty."

Justin has a babysitter, Megan. She plays with Justin and takes him to different activities. And he has a specially trained dog named Pivy who goes places with him. When he's at a store, Justin wanders off a lot, but if he holds on to Pivy, he can't wander off.

Faith & Justin

Justin and I are different from other sisters and brothers 'cause we don't fight much. We play. We play on Justin's swing and we blow bubbles outside. Justin likes it when I make big bubbles. When we go to the swimming pool, my dad picks us up and throws us into the water. Justin can hold his breath for a really long time. We toss sticks in the water, and Justin can pick up all the sticks.

When Justin says, "Be alone, Faith," that means he wants me to leave him alone. And when he says, "Your turn," he means it's *his* turn. He gets those words mixed up, but I understand what he's saying.

Justin and I like to blow bubbles.

I'm eleven and my sister Raquel is nine. She has autism. My parents told me that autism is not a disease. But it makes Raquel different from other kids. She doesn't look different. She only acts different. She's in her own world, and she doesn't really know how to speak. Some kids ask her how old she is. She just walks away. When she's mad or upset and she has a tantrum, people cover their ears. If she didn't have autism, she could say what's wrong.

My mom teaches Raquel at home. They do arts and crafts, and Raquel has a board with pictures on it. She points to things she wants on the board, like an apple or a banana. And she's really good at puzzles. I hope she learns to read because

Paloma & Raquel

I love to read. I love Harry Potter. *Harry Potter and the Order of the Phoenix* is my favorite Harry Potter book.

Most of my friends have younger sisters and they fight with them a lot. Raquel and I don't fight. We like to roller blade. She can go a lot faster than I can. If we were having a race, she'd win.

Raquel really likes our little brother, Bobby. She runs around the house and he follows her. My friends like to play with Bobby. He's only three but he talks more than Raquel. Sometimes when Raquel's making a lot of noise, he says, "Raquel, be quiet!"

Raquel doesn't look different from other people.

Rachael loves eating snow!

My sister Rachael is older than me. She's nine and I'm seven. She has autism, and she can't talk.

In the summer Rachael and I go to the beach. We play in the sand and swim in the water. In the winter we play outside. I like to run around in the snow and lie down in it. Rachael likes to eat the snow. I tell her to save some for me.

When Rachael comes in my room, she puts a chair against the bureau so she can reach my unicorn stuffed animal. Then she throws it on the floor. I think she does it because she wants to see if the unicorn can fly.

Olivia & Rachael

Every morning before school, Rachael and I go on the swing in our house. First Rachael does it. Then it's my turn. Sometimes we swing together. When we swing we like to listen to music. My mom puts on kids' songs and pop songs.

Rachael and I are in first grade. We go to different schools. Special teachers come to our house to help Rachael learn things, like her letters. She's really good at drawing. She makes flowers and the sun. I wish she could do a cartwheel and a handstand like me. Then we'd be twins.

My brother Shomik is different from other people. One time my friend and I were making puppets, and Shomik started screaming. I told my friend that Shomik has autism, and he screams very loud. When Shomik cries, I feel worried or scared that he might break a lamp. He did that one time. I wish he could talk.

When we go to the supermarket, sometimes Shomik gets upset and pulls things off the shelf and squeezes bottles. So my dad takes him to the car and stays with him while my mom and I buy groceries.

Shomik likes other kids, and he plays sports with them. He likes to play with Legos and sticky blocks.

Shumita & Shomik

Shomik and I play chase together. When we race, Shomik always wins. Maybe I'll win when I'm older.

Shomik goes to Countryside School, and he's in third grade. He has special teachers who help him make words and say things. And he goes to music class and sings songs with the teacher. I go to kindergarten and have play dates with my friends. There are some other kids at my school who have autism. I didn't know other people like Shomik, but now I do.

My big brother Shomik and I play together a lot.

I want to be the best brother to Mary Gwen that I can be.

Kids should know that autism is really challenging.
I think it would be frustrating to have autism. You'd say stuff and nobody could possibly understand you. I wish Mary Gwen could talk. It would be nice to hear what she has to say. She could tell us if something hurts instead of hitting us.

Mary Gwen likes me. I know because she smiles when she sees me. I want to be the best brother I can be. But sometimes I get ticked when Mary Gwen hits and screams.

Christian & Mary Gwen

It's hard because you don't know why she does it. But she's doing the best she can. She's trying very, very hard to learn. She goes to a school for kids with autism, and she works with play therapists who come to our house and go places with us.

Mary Gwen absolutely loves swimming, in any kind of water. She's actually a pretty good swimmer now. She can go for hours in the pool or in the ocean.

Autism has helped us to become a better family. It teaches us patience and understanding. If you see a kid on the street with autism, don't yell at her if she's doing something wrong. She can't help it. You should respect people with autism for who they are.

For Luke and Arie, two great kids!—O.S.

For Lisa—S.V.

Library of Congress Cataloging-in-Publication Data

Shapiro, Ouisie.
Autism and me : sibling stories / by Ouisie Shapiro ; photographs by Steven Vote.
p. cm.
ISBN 978-0-8075-0487-1
1. Autistic children—Juvenile literature. 2. Autistic children—Family relationships—
Juvenile literature. 3. Brothers and sisters of people with disabilities—Juvenile literature.
I. Title.
RJ506.A9S523 2009   618.92'85882—dc22   2008031700

The design is by Carol Gildar.

For more information about Albert Whitman & Company,
visit our web site at www.albertwhitman.com.